AF802955

Hello Michael,

Please, enjoy this copy of our latest book.

Looking forward to our next meeting - Cheers!

Christian

IS MY MONEY *OK?*

IS MY MONEY *OK?*

EMPOWER YOUR CONFIDENCE
TO HELP DREAMS HAPPEN

Ralph Antolino, Jr.

Investment Advisory Services offered through AA Financial Advisors, LLC

Antolino & Associates, Inc.
contact@antolino.com
https://www.antolino.com/

"Is My Money OK?", Ralph Antolino, Jr. —1st ed.

CONTENTS

INTRODUCTION

Congratulations. Since you decided to read this, you probably have already had some successes in your life. A good education. An above-average job, career, or business interest. You probably believe that there are opportunities you've yet to capture and dangers you are not fully prepared for. You want and expect more out of your future. A financial "to-do" list may be on your desk or in your head. Is that list getting done at the rate you'd like? If not, do you have too many urgent and important things to do that cause you to procrastinate? Or, do you lack the confidence to move forward?

Maybe you don't have a "system" that keeps you in charge of directing your current advisors to help you. Are these advisors optimizing your finances? Do your advisors communicate ideally between themselves and you? If not you are likely not capturing the best opportunities nor doing anything to avoid your big potential dangers. Is there a specific financial hurdle on your mind? Such as retirement planning, the sale of a business, larger philanthropic gifts, or helping extended family. Are you as clear as you can be with yourself and those who are trying to help you make financial progress in your life? Do you have a collection of advisors working for you and you wonder if they all really understand what is important to you? Are these advisors working together to get *you* what *you* want?

We wrote this book to show you that those equipped with a good "system" accomplish a great deal more. You're probably a successful individual who likes to push to be better. If you can help it, you want your future to be brighter than your past.

To some degree, you are driven, determined, and ambitious. If this sounds like you, then using a system for getting "ultra" clear about your vision of your future and how to best connect your finances to that future has the potential to exponentially accelerate your progress. Others have found that this progress came in ways that they never considered. Once you are clear on the steps and the process, then you become confidently empowered to better communicate with and control those best capable and interested in helping you achieve your dreams, goals, and ambitions.

Rather than merely "patching up holes," addressing problems as they come up, what if you employed a system that proactively sought ways to help you unite your finances to your deepest passions and drives in the world?

What if your finances were more effectively connected to and in support of your reason for being alive on this Earth? What if your money helped you fulfill your life's mission?

In this book, we'll introduce The UltraVision System®. It is truly a one-of-a-kind process designed to help you preserve, build, and transfer your wealth optimally. You will learn how to become more clear with yourself, your spouse, and those who support your dreams, goals, and ambitions. See why weak math models lead to poor decision-making. You will learn what a good math model is and how it Empowers Confidence™ and clarity about your vision. This all happens as you better connect your finances to the social, emotional, and spiritual dimensions of your life. Through the steps of the process, you will see how The UltraVision System® helps make your dreams come true.

With The UltraVision System®, your creative thinking doesn't stop at the numbers. Your financial decisions should help you better live the life you want to live. Your "wealth" is about more than "numbers". It can help facilitate what is important to you. With a quality Letter of Intent, you begin to empower your confidence. That is, confidence that:

- You are taking the right steps at the right time to get where you want to go, the way you want to get there.
- Your peace of mind is not elusive.
- The memories you make with those you love and care about will be long-lasting.
- The impact you can have during your lifetime on those around you.
- The legacy of your values, both philosophical and financial will reflect what you really want.

Most people, without thinking about it further, are content with the transactional or surface-level thinking that advisors tend to provide. They silo their lives to get their taxes done, invest their money, and put their insurance in place. Their advisors usually talk about idle chatter and numbers and leave it at that. This book is not for most people...

Our firm cares deeply about the few great people who want more.

Getting more out of your finances should translate to getting more out of life.

The people who never rest on their laurels. The people who always ask, "What next? How can I be even more successful? How can I accomplish an even bigger, more challenging goal?"

It's our mission to help *the few great people* that we are privileged to introduce to The UltraVision System® to make their dreams come true from the multiple dimensions of their family wealth.

This process begins with clarity. What do you want out of life? What impact do you want to have? What values do you hold dear?

After a thorough exploration of who you are and what your goals are, we use sophisticated wealth models to design a new plan that will get you where you want to go.

For the select few, we act as facilitators and advisors for life. We remind them and help them take the right steps to fulfill their UltraVision. We're like Jiminy Cricket on Pinocchio's shoulder with a gentle "nudge" and friendly, regular support.

If you aspire to empower your confidence and the capability of your finances to better support your dreams, goals, and ambitions, in a unique and more powerful way, then read on.

CHAPTER 1

Am I Okay?

Every client we meet comes to us with an itch.

The "itch" is a problem, financial in nature, that a person perceives that they have.

Itches come in all shapes and colors. A few examples include:

- ☐ Will I be able to live the lifestyle I want after I sell my business?
- ☐ How do I optimize the after-tax sale proceeds from my business?
- ☐ How do I reduce the ever-increasing amount of taxes I seem to be paying?
- ☐ Are my income-producing assets aligned to get me what I want out of life?
- ☐ How can I simplify the increasing complexity accompanying my financial success?
- ☐ Are my children prepared to receive what we have accumulated and may leave for them in after-tax proceeds?

- ☐ I have heard there are ways to trade tax dollars for philanthropy and end up wealthier in the process. Can you show me how that is done?
- ☐ Am I on track to being financially independent someday?
- ☐ I hope my existing advisors have helped me in every way possible, but I wonder what dangers or opportunities a fresh set of eyes might uncover for my situation.
- ☐ Would moving to another country help me keep more of my hard-earned money?
- ☐ Our tax system is bewildering. Am I avoiding my fair share of the dangers and capturing the opportunities that good tax planning may offer?

Do you recognize yourself in any of these itches? Take a moment to check off the box next to any "itch" you currently have.

Most people have one driving itch—the itch that likely motivated you to pick up this book, thinking, "Will this finally help me solve my problem once and for all?" Alongside this core itch, you likely have many others on your mind.

But usually, these "itches" are just the tip of the iceberg of a person's financial needs. Maybe their concern about their investment plan is their most urgent, top-of-mind problem, but lurking behind this "itch" are other worries.

If someone comes to me saying, "I need help with my IRA," I know that there are deeper concerns below the surface.

After asking a few questions, I find out more. This client is nearing retirement and anxious about having the right plan in place. His aging mother is sick, and he wants to ensure he can support her. His adult son wants to start a business and has asked his father for financial help to launch it.

This client thinks, “I’ve built a successful business and my wife and I have a nice lifestyle, but will I be able to sustain the life I want to live when I sell the business? Can I afford to help my mother and my son if I’m no longer working? Will there be anything left in my estate for my family, or will I have to use it all in retirement? I wanted to leave money to my grandkids so they could attend their dream colleges... Would that be possible? How in the world can I accomplish everything I want to do for my family and still retire when I want to?”

These questions spiral and spiral until the client’s true problem comes out. It isn’t just about the IRA... It’s about this client’s fear that his current retirement plan won’t allow him to live the life he wants to live.

At the bottom of every itch is an unspoken question: “Am I okay?”

Will I have enough money? Am I making the right decisions about my investments? Am I saving enough? What will my retirement look like? Am I using the right financial formula? How do I keep track of all my accounts? Am I using the right advisor?... All of these questions boil down to ”Am I okay?”

Are your finances prepared to weather the possible disasters you could face? Could a personal, unexpected lawsuit pull your financial security rug from under you? What if you die suddenly? Will your survivors have enough money to maintain their lifestyle if that happens? What if someone sues your business to smithereens? Will your money be safe from creditors, or are you at risk of losing everything you've worked for? Will the wheels fall off the track if you face a worst-case scenario? Will you be okay?

For some people, the "Am I okay?" question is more like "Am I optimized?" These people aren't worried about a worst-case scenario… Their fear is more like a fear of missing out. They wonder if there are strategies or tools their current advisor hasn't implemented, and they want to ensure the plan they have is the best of the best.

I like to say that all of our clients have "a future brighter than their past." We work with successful people who are never content to rest with the success they have—they always want to accomplish more. That mindset translates to finances as well. Why settle for the plan you made years ago when you could explore today whether or not there are better options out there?

One of the most common "itches" I hear about is the sale of a business. Most business owners put much effort into building, growing, and scaling their business… Then, when they decide they'd like to pull some equity out of the business or transfer it to family, they realize they have no idea how to exit the business in the best way possible. They wonder, "Should I sell my business? Should I find a successor? Should

I gift it to my family somehow? I'd like to give some part of this to employees, but I don't see how they could possibly afford it or get a loan to do it. How can I get the highest possible net when I sell? How can I ensure that the business I worked for decades to build can survive beyond me?"

Sometimes, with the sale of a business, people get hung up on a number for their selling price. They may think, "I can get $50 million for my business…I won't settle until I find a seller willing to give me that." Often, due to inexperience in selling a business, they lose track of terms, conditions, and taxes. They are fixated only on the big number. In the end, they get less than what they might have received with a more holistic approach.

It can be lonely running a business. Especially if you're trying to sell. There may not be anyone in your organization you can confide in or turn to for objective advice. Overwhelmed by the options and unsure of what approach to take, selling a business can be one of the most frustrating and confusing itches for an owner to contend with.

No matter which itch is driving you crazy, it's likely that your spouse is feeling the effects of the itch, too…

Good relationships are built on delegation—divide and conquer. In most relationships, one spouse deals with the finances while the other spouse handles other responsibilities. This works well for balancing responsibility in a relationship, but the result is that one spouse has no clue what's going on with the family finances.

Usually, the "non-money" spouse is happy to let the other spouse handle everything and doesn't want to bother thinking about investments and taxes. But in the back of their mind, the "non-money" spouse is nervous... The unknown can be frightening, and to your spouse, your finances are a huge unknown. They may not even know the full picture of everything you have, and this lack of knowledge can cause them to have thoughts like, "Will we have enough money to travel when we retire?" Most of all, your spouse fears your death. If you pass away suddenly and your spouse has to take over the financial responsibilities, he or she will feel out of their depth.

Your spouse is also thinking, "Am I okay?" just the same as you are. But sometimes, this question can be more frightening to your spouse because he or she has less familiarity with the ins and outs of your current plan.

The 9-Dot Puzzle

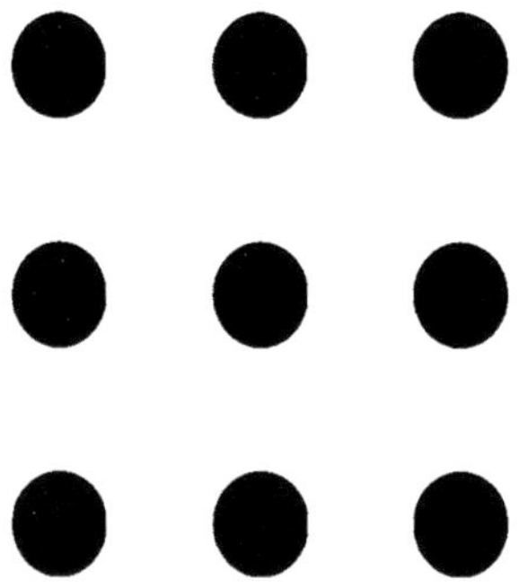

Can you connect all 9 dots using only 4 continuous straight lines?

It's challenging, right?

Imagine that these 9 dots represent components of your financial world. Maybe one dot is your taxes, one dot is your business succession plan, one dot is your spouse's dream to own a beach house in retirement, one dot is a sick relative you're supporting, one dot is an investment opportunity you have, one dot is a lawsuit your business is involved in, and so on. Your challenge is to connect every dot so that all of your wants and needs are fulfilled and all of your obstacles are overcome. You can't leave any dot unconnected because doing so will have consequences for you and your family. You need to connect the dots and have every part of your financial world working in harmony.

The problem is that your current advisors are likely each focused on only one dot. Your attorney is focused on ensuring a lawsuit doesn't hurt your business. Your CPA Is focused on meeting this year's tax deadline. Your retirement planner is focused on your investment portfolio and doesn't know much about what's going on with your business. Each of these professionals is great at handling one dot in the puzzle. But nobody is helping you look at and manage the whole picture. Your dots are never connected. Each part of your financial world becomes siloed, and this leaves you unable to achieve everything you want to achieve because you're missing a holistic, strategic perspective.

And this isn't your fault… For many who have reached a level of success in life, they find that their financial life has grown in complexity over time. Often, it gets to a point where it becomes difficult to keep up with everything. You simply may not have the time to get your arms around all of the financial pieces.

When you're young you often don't have much to worry about. You have a paycheck and a checkbook and are just beginning to save money to buy a car or a house. But as you grow older and become more successful in your career, things become more complicated.

When you begin to add in owning a business, real estate, investment accounts, and more, things can grow to the point where you don't have as tight a handle on things as you might like.

As you become successful, the added responsibilities and obligations often pull your attention away from your finances. We find that for many successful people, their day-to-day grows into a hectic schedule of running a business, sitting on boards, speaking at conferences, or hosting networking dinners. You hope, "My advisor is handling everything." You may feel that you don't have time to pay attention to all the moving parts of your financial world, but you begin to wonder if your current advisor is optimizing your portfolio.

It can feel overwhelming…

It's like the game "Whack-A-Mole." When you began your career, maybe you only had two or three moles to manage.

Now, you might have 30, and it feels like you can never keep them all under control. There's always a fire to put out somewhere or an urgent opportunity to seize. Before long, your financial strategy falls by the wayside as you focus on all of the other facets of your life.

While everyone wishes there was a clear answer to any "itch," the reality is that there's no one "right way" to solve a financial problem or optimize a portfolio. To accomplish that, we need a skillfully selected combination of the available tools and strategies that best fit your unique situation. The more complex your situation, the more difficult this is to do. You can't do it alone... Many people try to manage their own finances, but become overwhelmed or simply busy and let things fall by the wayside. But your finances are too important to take a backseat... You need someone to manage them for you and take a holistic view of your life, your desires, and your challenges to determine which specific strategies would best apply to you.

We need to ensure your finances are working as one cohesive whole driving you toward the destination you desire.

Your money is like water. If you pour water into your hands, and you don't cup your hands, it's gone. Do you cup your hands? Even if you do, water is hard to hold in your hands. It quickly seeps through the cracks. What if you used something better than your hands to capture the opportunities you have for a secure future?

In the next chapter, we'll explore how you can move from complexity to clarity, and connect the dots in the puzzle.

CHAPTER 2

Complexity to Clarity

Congratulations! You're successful. If you've read this far, you probably have a good income, are paying taxes, have some discretionary cash flow, and want to make the most of it today and in the future.

As a byproduct of this success, you get…complexity from a growing list of "acquisitions" (toys, homes, investments, benefits, offspring, businesses, relationships, etc.) all of which lead to a squeeze on your time. That squeeze turns into a lack of clarity and confusion.

If you own a business, you have many accounts, and you have multiple advisors. As time goes on, you may find yourself in more complex situations that involve greater amounts of discretionary cash flow, bigger tax bills, and more moving parts of your financial landscape.

This is where there is a real danger. I find that many people suffer from little to no coordination between their various advisors. Often CPAs, attorneys, insurance agents, and investment advisors or brokers are siloed. Even if they know each other in passing, most clients do a poor job of coordinating these various advisors so they are working on the whole picture together. Nor do they reach a deeper relationship with each advisor in which the advisor understands what they really want in life beyond a single financial transaction.

If you're like most of the people who seek our help, your advisors are likely not engaged emotionally with you and your family and the diverse goals and objectives you are juggling. These advisors are doing what they see as their job. That doesn't mean they're bad advisors—they're just operating by the norms of their respective industries and the expectations you have set for them. All of your current advisors work in different disciplines. The trouble is, your itch may be much bigger than any individual discipline. You need someone who understands the big picture–where you want to go in life–and thinks about your finances holistically and can help you manage your advisors effectively.

Your CPAs likely don't have time to consider the big picture. They're deadline-driven. And you need them to be—it's to your benefit to have them focused on meeting tax deadlines. But this means you can't rely on them to "zoom out" and plan for your future. It is the reality of their industry today.

Likewise, your legal professionals are focused on the present. They're putting out fires and generally don't consider your life's purpose or what you want over the next 30 years.

Attorneys have some of the most chaotic and overwhelming workloads of any industry. It's only natural that this means some things fall through the cracks. They don't have time to chase you down or micromanage you.

I can't count the number of times a new client has given us their estate plan to review. Usually, it comes in a big envelope an inch or two thick. I'm shocked when it happens, and it happens often that the documents are expertly prepared, but unsigned. Big money spent, no plan in force.

Somewhere, the client has a letter from the lawyer saying, "Come into our office to sign the documents." The client is busy running their business and forgets, and the lawyer gets busy with other cases and doesn't remind them. Months or years pass, and neither party realizes the mistake. It is not your lawyer's business to chase you.

Your CPAs and attorneys are always facing deadlines, and rarely have much time to help you to think strategically about the future. You pay them to handle your taxes and put out legal fires. But this means there's a gap on your team… You need someone to think strategically. If your key advisors aren't thinking strategically for you, that probably means you've got that role. Lonely, isn't it?

There is a growing industry of financial advisors. The one thing they have in common is that they would all like to manage your money. That tends to be the silo or focus of investment people. The interrelationship between your illiquid, non-marketable assets, your various cash flows, and the upside of the non-liquid opportunities that you have are not their focus. As a result, their silo doesn't help strategically either. Because you're so successful in your career, the demands of your role keep you too busy to pause and get your own clarity about what you want in life and how your finances can help you get there. It is a conundrum.

Your real problem isn't your "itch." It's that you have many itches. Also, you probably do not have a process to overcome them or a person responsible for doing so. You have the challenge of connecting nine dots, but your financial professionals can each only see one dot at a time, and you're often too busy to even look at the puzzle.

Many people think they have a financial advisor. But when you dig into it, how well do they know you? If you've hired an advisor who helps you for a half hour once every quarter, is that enough? How clearly are your advisors communicating the value they are creating and delivering to you?

Many people also have a financial plan in place already. But how well do you understand it? Are you sure it's helping you move toward your goals? And if you don't understand it, that's not your fault—that just means that your advisor hasn't put in the effort to build a relationship with you and ensure you understand your finances.

Many advisors are simply salespeople, and unfortunately for you, maybe they were just looking to make a sale… After the sale is made, they don't have much of an incentive to do more than the bare minimum for you. Often, even if you have a great, trustworthy advisor, you usually still won't have an advisor who understands your plan and how it relates to your life. Most advisors are numbers people, not relationship people. They may understand the numbers, but not what these numbers mean to you and your goals. The result is that you have a plan, but you don't understand how to use this plan to make decisions. The purpose of the plan is to have a framework to evaluate your actions and measure the value that alternative courses of action may deliver to you, your family, and your community.

Some people think, "I have a plan…" But what they have is just a retirement plan. It doesn't address legal issues, or taxes (outside the realm of a 401k or IRA), and it doesn't address long-term business plans. It's only a plan around primarily one (or at best, two) of the nine dots, and it's not coordinated with any of the others. Even if it's a decent plan, it's not a tool for making major progress.

A Person and A Process

Much of what we as financial consultants do involves "cleaning up chocolate messes." Overwhelmed by the complexity of their lives, successful individuals forget to keep up with the more tedious tasks that need to get done regularly to maintain their financial world. This disorganization compounds over the years until this person's finances are a big mess… It's nearly impossible to have clarity on your finances when you have a complex mess on your hands.

To move from complexity to clarity, you need a person and a process.

You can be that person if you want to, or you can engage an advisor. But I have a word of caution for the Do-It-Yourself-ers… As a driven person who likes to control his future, I can relate to your "can-do" attitude and your determination. These mindsets likely led you to the success you're enjoying today. But applying this same mindset to your finances as you grow from here might be a mistake. Studies have quantified the benefits of a high-quality advisor relationship, which can be as high as an extra 3% per year on your wealth. That can reduce the time it takes to double your money by 30% or more.

But maybe your desire to "do it yourself" isn't just about your entrepreneurial mindset. Some successful people have had bad experiences with an advisor of some sort and then shy away from another engagement for fear of repeating the same mistake. My advice for these people is to not let a bad experience with one advisor prevent you from finding an advisor who will actually help you get clarity on your finances. Likely, the advisor that frustrated you was working in a "silo" and was not engaging with the full picture of your 9-dot puzzle–or maybe they were a transactional advisor who was bent on selling you a specific product. Whatever the case, note your frustrations with that advisor and make sure your next advisor doesn't follow that pattern.

In business, a key component of growth is delegation. Businesses don't grow as one-person operations. Great businesses bring in qualified and skilled team members as they grow and experience compounding complexities. Why wouldn't you do the same with your finances and delegate to an expert so you can focus on other things? Isn't it smarter to free yourself up to use your intelligence and energy on something else? Yes, you certainly can do it yourself, but if you don't have to, why would you? If you ever hired an advisor who let you down, try again, you will be smarter and do better the next time. Just like with a bad hire in business... You wouldn't give up on filling a position just because the first person you hired didn't work. All employees are not perfect fits. You often have to try more than one to find the perfect fit.

You have one client—yourself. We have thousands. You're seeing the movie for the first time, but we've seen it thousands of times before. When it comes to managing your finances, you're learning. It will take you more time and effort to learn how to be successful at it than it would for a team that has done it thousands of times. And part of the learning process is making mistakes... Are you sure you want to make mistakes when your financial future is at stake and a mistake could be catastrophic? We know that you're a smart, capable person who could figure out how to manage your own finances, and you've probably done an above-average job to this point. However, all the best and brightest people throughout history have learned the value of delegation. If you delegate to the right advisor, the advisor can save you from potential mistakes and help you leverage more of your time to grow your business, develop your innovative ideas, or simply have more time to spend with friends and family.

So you have a person–your advisor. What's the process?

Our process is called The UltraVision System®. The UltraVision System® empowers entrepreneurial confidence through a time-tested feasibility study that assembles soft and hard facts into sophisticated math models, a family wealth Letter of Intent, and a prioritized list of options for major progress. This system is designed to connect your nine dots by taking an in-depth, holistic view of how your finances and your life intersect.

The 4 Dimensions of Wealth

We believe there are 4 dimensions of wealth: financial, emotional, social, and spiritual.

The financial dimension is a desire to be independent and to have the money to be able to do what you want to do. Most financial planning stops and starts with the financial dimension. The financial dimension is easy to discuss—it's A + B = C. It's mechanical and well-defined, but it's shallow. It tells us the numbers, but not what they mean to you. To most of our clients, it's the least important dimension because it doesn't get to the heart of what they want in life.

The social dimension is about helping others—your family and community. One client has a wife who never wanted to talk about money—until we connected it to the social dimension. She's active in her community and has goals she wants to accomplish in her charitable efforts. When we showed her that she could reduce her tax bill and send more of her money to her charitable causes instead of to the IRS, she finally became excited about financial planning. It's no longer just numbers to her–it's a way to contribute to causes she cares about and be a leader in her community. After decades of letting her husband handle everything related to money, she's on fire and totally engaged about her finances.

The emotional dimension is about feeling good about what you're doing. We as humans tend to make decisions emotionally and then defend our decisions with logic. If people don't emotionally feel that a financial decision makes sense, they won't do it. Emotions are complicated, very personal, totally undefined, and much more difficult to discuss. Emotions take most advisors way out of their comfort zone.

Some people raise their eyebrows when we mention the spiritual dimension of wealth—what you believe in. But I can't tell you how many times I've mentioned faith to a client and they've said, "Oh, good, finally someone asked me and is willing to talk about that." Many advisors are uncomfortable talking about faith, but it's important to understand what someone believes in when making important decisions. A person's values will impact how they want to use their money. Your spiritual beliefs ought to be woven into your plan so you can ensure your money is being used in a way that supports your values. Tying your money to your value system is your opportunity to do that.

Most people treat these four dimensions as a baseball diamond. They touch each base, but they never try to connect them cohesively. With this compartmentalized approach, usually, something ends up being out of balance. One of the circles may end up being bigger than the others, or one circle may be excluded completely.

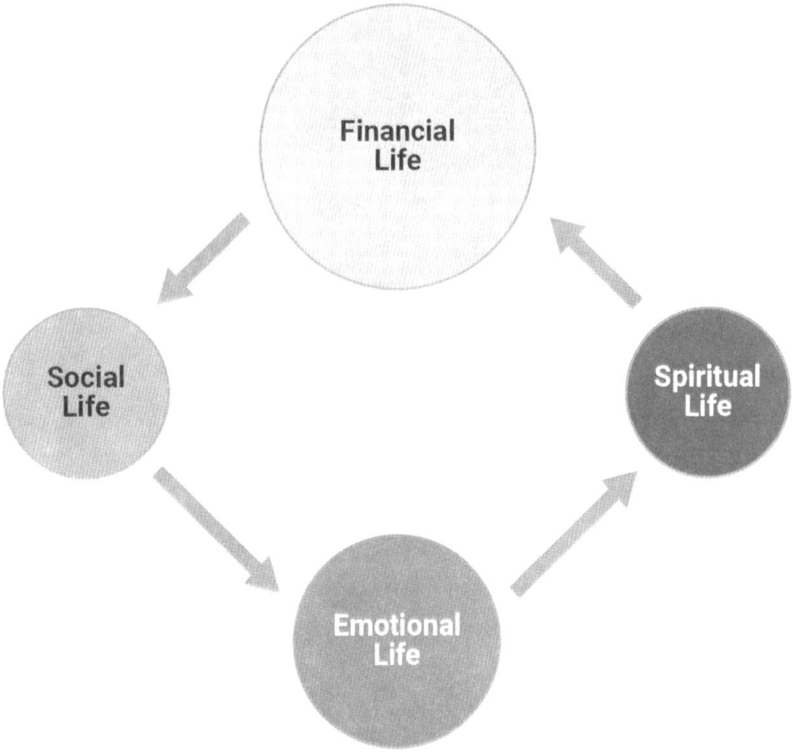

Where is my life's purpose in this?

The UltraVision System® tries to expand the circle of each of these dimensions and find their intersection. That intersection is what we call your passion. What's the fire within you? What's the driving force of your life? That's the intersection of all of the circles.

The question at the center of every life is "What's my purpose? Why am I doing this?" In our retreat, we help people answer this question if they haven't already. Then, as advisors, our job is to help you synergize the four dimensions of wealth around your life's purpose.

Writer George Bernard Shaw said, "This is the true joy in life, being used for a purpose recognized by yourself as a mighty one."

When your plan connects all four dimensions of wealth, keeping up with your finances no longer becomes a chore…

It becomes exciting because it's your passion. It's no longer just about the numbers—it's about your purpose.

For example, we helped a client trade tax dollars for a philanthropic cause he's passionate about. His rural community had very poor emergency medical services. Watching his wife die prematurely from an accident that most people with good emergency medical services would survive haunted him. When planning his estate, he felt strongly that he didn't want to spoil his kids or make life too easy for them by just leaving them large sums of money. He wanted them to have a rewarding life of learning and to be successful. He wanted a structure that provided his children with a "hand up" and not merely a "hand out". Inheriting his philosophical values along with his financial values was very important to him. Instead of paying the maximum in taxes, he learned, with a good math model, that he could redirect those dollars to make a significant impact on his part of the world. He saw he could save lives and provide comfort to thousands in his area by bringing up to modern standards the equipment and personnel needed to provide quality care to his friends, family, and customers in a large geographic area. He did this by strategically redirecting his tax dollars to this cause. When we focused his plan around this purpose, his planning sessions became invigorating. Managing his finances was no longer a headache-inducing drudgery to check off his to-do list. It was infused with optimism and excitement because we were helping him make an impact for a cause he cared deeply about while instilling his children with the values he held dear.

A plan that focuses merely on the financial dimension doesn't answer the question, "How am I going to be remembered when I'm gone? What's my legacy?"

There's a quote from Ernest Becker that says, "What man really fears is not so much extinction, but extinction with insignificance." People want to know that they've left a trace after they're gone. Finding your life's mission and connecting it to your finances is important and psychologically valuable.

After we get clarity about what the four dimensions of wealth mean to you, we'll begin a process of optimizing your finances to support your purpose. We'll start with the big rocks—usually, when we start with the big rocks, the little rocks take care of themselves. The big rocks tend to be your business, liquidity, and taxes. Then, we'll move to the next biggest rock and the next, and the next—until your finances are totally organized and in support of your passion.

CHAPTER 3

The UltraVision System®

The UltraVision System® is a multidimensional planning process that begins with the end in mind.

Successful planning is much more than simply looking at a net worth statement, tax tables, and running the numbers. As covered in the previous chapter, it's about connecting the 4 dimensions of wealth to help you fulfill your life's purpose. The UltraVision System® was built to help you get clarity around the four dimensions of wealth and how they interrelate in your life.

The UltraVision System® starts with an engagement agreement custom-built for your situation. It will have a focus on an "itch" you have to improve your situation from a net cash flow and/or asset accumulation perspective. Just as important as the itch identification, the process explores, identifies, and quantifies dangers and opportunities around that itch that could derail or enhance your chances of success. In the end, upon your "graduation," you will have a greater sense of confidence that the next steps you take are well coordinated to improve the chances of achieving your dreams, goals, and ambitions.

When you engage, you will shortly thereafter receive a set of checklists to complete in preparation for your retreat. One list of questions deals with an easy way for you to organize your financial information which we call the "hard facts." The other checklist is focused exclusively on the "soft facts," which have nothing to do with money. This checklist is an opportunity for you (and your spouse if appropriate) to explore where you've come from, what and who has influenced what you have become, and where you want to go from the strategic and philosophical aspects of wealth. These questions will help you explore the emotional, spiritual, and social aspects of your wealth. These are the dimensions that add great value and confidence. These are the aspects given short shrift by most advisors, yet our clients tell us these are the most important aspects to them. We find it difficult to care deeply and put ourselves in your shoes unless we understand these confidential and important dimensions of your family wealth.

Surveys show the vast majority of families spend much more time planning their vacations than thinking about their finances. We took that to heart and designed a retreat process that can include an "Envisioncation." This mini trip typically takes a married couple (sometimes a single person or just one spouse) off to a very nice resort. The purpose of this mini trip is to do some homework, usually in the two-hour range, and come prepared to focus for the best part of two days in a relaxing, special environment that is away from the pressures and distractions of your home town. Many clients stay a few extra days to continue contemplating and enjoying each other's company thinking more about their future.

The retreat is designed to get clients *really clear* about where they've come from, where they are today, and most importantly, where they want to go in the future from a philosophical and strategic perspective (emotional, social, and spiritual values) in addition to what they want their money to do for them. Most graduates claim this retreat or "Envisioncation" is the most valuable piece of the process to them. It not only clarifies their thinking about the future but delivers a special, never-forgotten experience that enhances their confidence about future big decision-making. We have taken clients on houseboat trips, race car driving adventures, exotic island experiences, and numerous other special events at the "advanced" level of the process.

Many people figure out how to make money adding value to others' lives, but are not clear in their vision of what they want to do with it. This conundrum has been explored in many ways in the past. For example, in the famous musical, South Pacific, Bloody Mary tells Lt. Joe Cable, "If you no hava a dream, how you maka dreama come true?" Also, when Alice meets the Cheshire Cat in Alice in Wonderland she asks him "Which road should I take?" The cat asks, "Where do you want to go?" When she replies, "I don't know", the cat says "If you don't know where you want to go, any road will get you there." Do you want to take "any road" and just get "somewhere?" Or do you want to get an UltraVision about what you want and how to get there?

It is much more fulfilling to be clear with yourself first, then with others who support you about what you want and to be pursuing it, than to be meandering through life on "any road." The goal of the retreat is to produce a Letter of

Intent that memorializes a bit of your family history (where you have come from) and where you want to go from the perspective of each of the four dimensions of wealth. It is a lightning rod that attracts great ideas and deflects ideas inconsistent with what you have decided you want.

The Letter of Intent is the initial deliverable or benchmark result of The UltraVision System®. This letter is a tangible articulation of what you want in life—and how the four dimensions of wealth intersect to form your purpose. It covers your values and virtues, your influences, and your life's purpose.

A famous university, we are told, performed a study with their graduates over a thirty-year period. The university wanted to know why some of its graduates were wildly successful while others floundered in life. What was the difference between these graduates? And how could some students attend one of the most elite universities in the world and still not find success?

The study found that the students who did the worst graduated, then beat their chests, and said, "Here I am world, you owe me." They didn't have any clear goals or ambitions, instead believing that success would be automatic due to their educational pedigree. Reality flattened them like a pancake.

The next most successful group was those who graduated with dreams, goals, and ambitions.

The second most successful group had goals, dreams, and ambitions… And put them into writing. Psychologists know that when humans commit an idea to writing, the chance of its success increases exponentially.

The most successful group had goals, put them into writing, and shared them with people who were supportive of their achievement. This is why this first step, the retreat, and Letter of Intent development, is so critical.

When a goal is in writing, the brain takes it more seriously—and when you have someone supportive who can remind you of your goals, you're more likely to hold yourself accountable.

That's how the UltraVision System® works. The UltraVision System® helps you clarify your goals. You craft a Letter of Intent to memorialize your goals in writing. Then, over the years, we're by your side to remind you of what your goals are when you forget them or stray from the path. We help you break the steps for achievement into bite-sized pieces so you can easily focus and progress.

In the Letter of Intent, you'll answer the question "What do I/we want?" We can't answer that question for you—only you know the answer deep down. But we can help guide you to the answer within you by asking questions, discussing, and helping you develop your top ideas until you get clarity about what you want.

Some of the questions we may ask to guide you may include:

- Who influenced you to become who you are today?
- What ideas/forces influence what you value the most in your life?
- What has to happen to you in your life, 36 months from now, in your mind's eye (your UltraVision) for you to feel happy about your progress, both personally and professionally, with respect to your finances?
- What's important about money to you?
- What are the dangers you see or feel facing you that could disrupt your vision?
- What are the opportunities you see that excite you in your future that may or may not require financial resources?
- What do you really care about?
- You have probably worked hard to get to this point in your life. What did you do this for and what do you want to do with the rest of your life?
- In what ways do you want to make the world a little bit better?
- If you could trade the dollars you spend on taxes for philanthropy, what causes would you want to support with those dollars? How would doing this make a difference in your life and/or the lives of your family and community?
- Would you like to use your income tax payments to redeem or unleash some equity in your business?

We'll also show you a list of values and ask you to identify which three you value the most.

Sometimes, when answering these questions, spouses realize that their answers differ from each other. This can be incredibly insightful. Without taking the time to reflect on these questions and get clear on the answers, most spouses might move through life assuming they both share the same values and desires. By communicating their answers to each other at the retreat, spouses can get on the same page about how they want to use their wealth.

Many come to a deeper appreciation of how they differ in ways that complement and strengthen each other and their relationship. They also almost always find a way to accomplish the important goals that each one wants to accomplish, connecting the nine dots within the rules and limitations of the game.

An UltraVision Success Story

A highly compensated executive at a Fortune 500 company had climbed through the ranks and was now in a leadership role. She had a nice base salary, extremely large bonuses, and was accumulating wealth at a rapid pace. Her bonuses, combined with her stock options, made her wealthier than she'd imagined she'd ever be.

We were introduced to her by a fellow corporate executive who had success with us. At first, she was a little skeptical of the process. We encouraged her to engage us in a feasibility study, which she and her husband did. To do the study, we went on a retreat to New York City, where we met with her and her husband over two days. We also got to see her actor son perform in a play, which was a real treat.

As a result of the retreat and our study of the hard facts and soft facts, this woman and her husband uncovered several hidden dangers and some significant opportunities. Years later, they both recalled that the retreat itself was one of the best experiences of their married life. They had never taken an extended period like that to focus on how their finances connected with their lives, the lives of their family, and ultimately, their community. The epiphany they had was seeing an array of things they could do. They also were exposed to dangers they were not thinking about. For example, her executive benefit plan covered 60% of her compensation. However, in the fine print (which we studied for her) the plan capped the benefit at $5,000 a month. This was of course only a teeny percentage of what she was making. As a result, we helped the company install an executive disability program to cover the executives at a much more appropriate level. This added to their sense of confidence and security moving forward.

The math model gave them confidence in what they could spend on their lifestyle while not taking away from their future financial security. A sense of balance and appropriateness came through to them.

Their wealth transfer plan was put in place when they had young children. Their children were now out earning their own way through life, getting married, and having families of their own, and the wealth transfer plan was now inappropriate. We helped them strategically think through how they wanted to help these children make their way during their lifetime and thereafter.

As a result of the success they had in the plan, this executive has been instrumental in introducing us to new people who were in situations similar to hers, moving up the corporate chain and thinking they're okay when they've never really looked closely or had an independent third party examine their situation from an unemotional, detached perspective with the benefit of lots of other experiences behind their belt. The real epiphany, again, was the retreat. They had no idea the benefits that come from focusing on their situation in a structured, facilitated manner.

CHAPTER 4

Unpacking Your Brighter Future

The people we work with all have a future brighter than their past. They want something better than their status quo.

You want something, and even if you don't know exactly what you want or how to get it, you're driven and you're willing to put in the work to get there. And what you want is bigger than "more money." You see money as a tool to help you get what you really want.

Pilots have a saying, "It's dangerous to get fat, dumb, and happy." If you're flying a plane, and everything's going great—you're on course, you have plenty of fuel—you'll let your guard down. The second you let your guard down and sit relaxed in the cockpit with a smile on your face, not being attentive, something may go wrong and you won't be prepared to fix it in time.

In the business world, "fat, dumb, and happy" is the executive or business owner who is content to stop growing the business as soon as it provides them with enough money to live a comfortable life. Then, the business turns south or he or she sells the business with a weak math model. As a result, the business owner's lifestyle has to change dramatically. Life is no longer quite as fun.

Our clients are not the kind of people who become "fat, dumb, and happy." They don't rest on their laurels. Each time they accomplish a goal, it only fills them with more energy and drive to pursue a bigger goal. They always want to make the world a little bit better.

There's an old clip of Barbara Walters interviewing Howard Hughes, who at the time of the interview was the wealthiest guy in the world. She asked him, "So Mr. Hughes, how much more money does a guy like you need?" He leaned over and said, "Just a little bit more."

All of our clients have that mindset in common, they want just a little bit more, whether we're talking about family happiness, money, the growth of their business, or impact in their communities. Our clients are not merely satisfied with the status quo or merely being secure. They're comfortable being uncomfortable. They know that no success is final, and they want to push their success further and further.

Yet, success means different things to different people. That's why we spend so much time getting to know our clients. We want to know what success means to you. We take you through a process that gets you to a state of clarity. In the end, you will have a clear vision of what a future brighter than your past looks like to you!

Articulating Your UltraVision

Do you have a clear vision of what you want? Most people have a foggy vision—or if they do have a clear vision, they aren't sure how to get to it.

You may not be crystal clear on what you want, but you know you want something. Or maybe you have an itch… You feel that something is not right with your finances, but you may not be clear on what that is. "Is it my retirement plan? Is it the equity of my business? Is it my spouse's spending habits?" You're looking for guidance or a sense of direction. We'll be the third party that gives you an objective perspective.

Or maybe you feel that everything's alright, but you want to know if there are any steps you can take to launch an even better and more secure financial future. You don't want to miss any opportunities, but you aren't sure what you're missing.

With The UltraVision System®, you'll get a clear view of where you are, where you want to go, and your choices for getting there. Our goal is to help you get your wants fulfilled.

We want to get to know you at a deep and meaningful level so we can help you get what you want and manage your financial affairs in a way that helps you get what you want. In short, we become *leverage* for busy, successful people to get more out of the financial "ingredients" they have accumulated in their lives so far.

To unpack your Ultravision, we'll look at both the soft facts and the hard facts. The hard facts are the numbers—where most financial planning stops and starts. For most clients, it is the most boring. We've had people tell us they'd rather go to the dentist than talk about their "numbers." The soft facts, by contrast, are your wants, non-financial values, and goals. The soft facts go beyond the numbers to tell us what your numbers could mean in your life. Your soft facts are: Where do I come from? What do I care about? What are my values? What do the dimensions of wealth mean to me? Where do I want to go?

This thinking will happen at a retreat during which we take you out of your day-to-day environment so you can get clarity on what you want.

You may be familiar with the psychological concept of "The Flow." You can't really get into the flow until you've had about 40 minutes of concentrated, uninterrupted effort on a specific topic.

This is why we do the retreat. If we met with you at your office or ours, we would never be able to get into the flow, let alone an "ultra" flow. People would knock on your door to interrupt you or you'd have to pause to take a call. Further, you'd be distracted by all of the "urgent and important" unexpected interruptions. Treat yourself to a retreat for your future.

To help you get greater clarity and perspective on your life, we have to take you out of your usual environment and give you time to examine your thinking, confirm your thinking, and clarify your thinking.

At the retreat, you can get into the flow and reflect on what you want in life. Most people have never taken the time to reflect on that in a dedicated way. They've likely thought about it in passing, but because they are successful, busy people, they've never had time to pause and think deeply about this question.

Before the retreat, you'll do the "homework" we described earlier by answering questionnaires about your dreams, goals, and ambitions and your hard facts–your assets, current spending, and current financial plan. Our team will make this preparation process easy for you by dividing it up into small bites you can digest easily. How do you eat an elephant? One bite at a time.

At the retreat, we discuss the answers to your questionnaire. Usually, we have further questions for clients after reading the questionnaire and will dig deep to uncover the truths underneath what's written on the questionnaire. We can't answer the big questions for you, but we can ask you questions and keep you focused and on track.

If you're married, the retreat will be done as a joint experience with your spouse. As a couple, you'll have the chance to get clear about the future you both want. If you are single or your partner does not want to participate, we have and can do them "solo." The best results come when couples participate together. It is truly a profound and unique experience worth doing together.

We also sometimes do family retreats after a plan is in place. It's important for your children to understand the choices you're making. We've had new clients come in after their parents have died and say, "If only I knew what Mom and Dad really wanted me to do with the estate..." By having these conversations with your kids while you're still alive, you can minimize their stress and confusion after you're gone. It can be powerful to have your family involved in conversations about what you want in life, and it can bring everyone closer together.

At the retreat, we'll uncover the biggest rocks—the goals that have the most leverage for you. You'll get clear on what those big goals are and what actions need to be taken to accomplish them.

Then, we'll craft your Letter of Intent, based on what you said you wanted. It is a documentation of your *intentions*–what you want in life. You'll review it and we'll revise it until it perfectly captures your goals for your future. Then, you'll sign it.

Before writing your Letter of Intent, you and your spouse may never have written down your dreams, goals, and ambitions in a comprehensive and organized way.

With the Letter of Intent, you get a clear articulation of your UltraVision–probably for the first time–and we get to understand who you are at a deep level. We care about you and are thinking all the time about what we can do to help you achieve your UltraVision.

We're paid to think for you. You're smart, hardworking, successful… This means that you don't have as much time as you'd like to think about your finances. It's powe rful when you add a team of people who are thinking ab out and advocating for your future while you're focused on your business, career, and family. This thinking is best done when armed with your Letter of Intent and your old plan's math model.

Sometimes we help clients solve problems that aren't even financial. Sometimes we introduce them to people in our network who could help them get closer to their goals or solve challenges they face. Our mission is to help make their dreams come true. If you "no hava a dream, howa you gonna make a dream come true?"

Now that we know what your dreams are, we'll do everything we can to help you achieve them. Helping you with your money plays a large part in that, but referring you to other people in our vast network is another way we deliver value.

We help make dreams come true… We don't make them come true all by ourselves—but through a proven and time-tested system, we help people preserve, build, and transfer wealth to achieve their dreams, goals, and ambitions.

The Importance of a Gentle Reminder (The Cricket Factor™)

A consultant using The UltraVision System® brings The Cricket Factor™ to their relationship with you. Remember the story of Pinocchio? Pinocchio had a dream of being a real boy. The fairy godmother gave him an easy recipe to follow for success. If it wasn't for the tiny cricket that gently reminded or nudged him of what he needed to do when he was distracted or veered off course, he never would have made his dream come true. We act as crickets on the shoulders of numerous Pinocchios. Here are a couple of examples of how that worked successfully for others.

The first client for The UltraVision System® was an old friend who was an accountant when I began working with him.

After we completed a review of the financial accounts we oversaw for him, as part of our regular process we asked him if there were any new goals or objectives he wished to pursue. We asked him, "What new do you want out of life? What else are you trying to accomplish now?"

He said, "My accounting job is decent…but what I really want is to get into real estate."

I didn't see him for a year, and we met up for our next annual review. I said, "How is the real estate going?"

He said, "Oh, I forgot about that… I still want to do it, but I haven't started yet."

Another year went by, and I asked him again how he was doing on his real estate goal.

Again, he said, "Yeah, I do really want to do that, but I've been busy and I haven't started yet."

I gently reminded him that if he never started on his goals, he would never accomplish them.

Years later, he was a successful real estate investor. "Congratulations," I told him.

"Well," he said, "I owe it all to you."

I said, "What are you talking about? I didn't have anything to do with this."

He said, "Remember when we had lunch, and you asked me what I wanted to do in life? I told you I wanted to pursue real estate, and then I never did anything to make that goal a reality. But you kept asking me about it, and after several years, your nudging made me realize I needed to act. After the last time you asked me, I went home and told myself that I wouldn't have lunch with you again until I could tell you that I made progress."

Notice how I didn't do anything in this story other than remind my friend of his goals. I couldn't pursue his goals for him… He had to take action and hold himself accountable. But in our busy lives, it can be difficult to look past the day-to-day struggles and remember the big-picture goal that you're moving toward. We can provide a gentle reminder that can make all the difference. Often, we can be the leverage you need to get things done through our team or by introductions to outside experts or relationships that might prove beneficial to you and your goals. The rest is up to you.

We recently had a restaurant owner tell us she owed tripling her business in three years to us. She claims we gave her the confidence to leave her old location and open a new and improved operation with her Letter of Intent, a great Math Model, and our Summary Opinion Letter which quantified and summarized the benefits of taking the risk of investing more into the business. That's The Cricket Factor™.

CHAPTER 5

Getting Clear on Where You Are Today

The Soft Facts:

The soft facts are who you are, what you care about, and the non-financial values that are most important to you and your family. These are uncovered in three important ways. The first step involves your answers to the "soft facts" questionnaires in preparation for your retreat. The second step involves your participation in the retreat.

Often, the "flow" that develops from focusing on the subject of "who am I and what do I want?" for more than just a few minutes can create epiphanies and moments of great clarity for participants. We make it easy for you to build on these moments by taking notes and memorializing your Letter of Intent. The third method for developing your soft facts is our process of regularly spaced discussion over extended periods that we call "cadence meetings."

A cadence is a regular nudge or small effort that, when compounded, leads to significant progress. These are the proverbial “bites of the elephant”. Think of it like a bicyclist putting regular effort on their pedals. In these sessions, we continue to work with you to learn more about your soft facts and how to best tie your financial resources to fulfilling your dreams, goals, and ambitions with respect to these soft facts. You too will gain greater clarity and confidence about what you value and want.

In the end, it seems that these soft facts are what matter most. We have found in our decades of experience that understanding these facts and their relationship to your finances makes a big, positive difference over extended periods of time.

The Hard Facts

The hard facts are where most advisors start and end their process. The hard facts are the numbers, the data, the information. The hard facts are important, but they’re not as important as great soft facts. They’re just the math, while the soft facts tell you what that math means for you and your family. But the hard facts do matter… And after unpacking what you want, we’ll take a look at the hard facts. We’ll quantify how much money you have, how much money you can expect to make in the future, how much you can expect to net after taxes, and how long you can expect to enjoy the lifestyle or rate of spending you desire. We’ll also prioritize what you want so we can get the most important things done first. Getting the hard facts and the soft facts right allows you to get a great grip on how realistic and feasible your various dreams, goals, and ambitions are. It also gets the data right to prepare and contrast the trajectory of your old plan against a set of new ideas that work together to form your new plan as validated by a quality math model that incorporates all the variables.

Lifestyle Definition

Then, if you don't already know it for sure, we'll figure out your lifestyle: what you're spending to live currently. Some call this your "burn rate" …the amount of cash you want to spend with no remorse on a regular basis.

Forensically, we can figure out what your lifestyle has been. We can look at your tax returns and investment accounts to determine how much money you made, how much money you saved, and whatever is left after taxes is lifestyle. Like it or not…

Once you begin working with us, we can analytically track everything you do with your money in great detail so we can coach you even better. We have a system we call The Wealth Management System™ where we can link all of your financial accounts to an aggregation system that summarizes the details of all the accounts. Many prospective clients say they've tried such systems but were not been able to get them to work or ran out of patience with them.

In your business, you likely know every detail about where your money goes. Why wouldn't you do the same with your personal finances? There is technology out there that can make it simple to track your income, expenses, purchases, sales, and credit cards to the nth degree. You could figure out how to do this yourself, or you could leverage our team of experts who can set this up quickly and confidentially and make it easier for you and your family to stay in charge of your finances with greater confidence and less time to do so. With clarity around your lifestyle, you can then make any changes you need to make to ensure you can accomplish your goals.

The "Fire Drill" Analysis

Next, we'll do a "fire drill" analysis around the topics involving preserving, building, and transferring your wealth. We read your legal documents and insurance contracts. Pretending the events you have prepared for in the past actually happen, we work the math and show you the results of your "old plan" under the list of scenarios you decided you wanted to be prepared for. The fire drill tests your current plan against your Letter of Intent. Does your current plan support your UltraVision? Or will you need to make changes to achieve your dreams?

For the "preserve" module, we'll test whether your current legal structures are set up to protect your various assets from liabilities. Are these legal structures well maintained? Do you have a corporate minute book? Is it up to date? Is your liability coverage appropriate? Many times, people set up insurance years ago and haven't updated it recently to reflect their changed financial and life circumstances. If you had a claim, would you be happy with the coverage you got? Do you know?

The "build" module is about your investments. Are your investments aligned with what you want to do from a risk-reward and investment-objective perspective? Many times, we'll find that business owners want to be as aggressive in their investments as they are in their business. We often find business owners, upon greater reflection, may be better suited to use their investments as their safety net. Many are "playing on the high wire." Their greatest opportunity for financial results is their business. If it doesn't work, or something unexpectedly bad happens, many would like their investments to be there for their recovery so they can play again. Their investments are truly a safety net in case they fall off the high wire of their business. The important question is, are you doing what you said you want to do with your investments? Are they consistent with your Letter of Intent? A quality feasibility study of your build plan will accomplish this.

With the "transfer" module, the system looks at how you share your wealth with others, both now and in the future. Do you have a gifting program during life that optimizes your dreams, goals, and ambitions, particularly concerning the opportunity for trading tax dollars for philanthropy and/or for avoiding the onerous estate tax at your death? At your death, there are only three places your money can go. Do you know for sure exactly how much will go to your family, the government, or charity? If you died today, where would your estate go and how much would it be worth? Are you happy with it, or do you need to make some changes to ensure more of your estate goes to your heirs or charity?

After the fire drill, we'll give you a summary opinion letter that summarizes where your plan is effective, where it could use course corrections, and where it could make some enhancements. We'll make conclusions just like a fire chief would when assessing the fire safety of a building.

A Succession Success Story

About five years ago, I was on a plane going from St. Thomas to Miami. My wife claimed the window seat that day, so I was stuck in the middle. The man next to me looked like a typical tourist, dressed very casually wearing a T-shirt, shorts, and tennis shoes. He did not come across as sophisticated or wealthy.

I had a book I wanted to read, but the man wanted to strike up a conversation. He started making small talk. "Do you go to St. Thomas very often?"

"I actually live on St. John," I said.

"You live on St. John?"

"Yes."

He kept asking questions, and I tried to make peace with the fact that I wasn't going to get to read my book on this flight. "How long have you lived there? Are you retired? What do you do?"

I told him I'm a tax attorney who does financial consulting for business owners.

He said, "Oh, man… I got tax problems."

He proceeded to tell me his tales of woe.

I realized I wasn't going to get much reading done so I closed my book and listened. We had a nice, long chat. It turns out you can't judge a book by its cover… This man, despite his appearance, was a wealthy business owner. He told me he takes pride when he travels to the various locations of his business, which employs over 500 people, that many of his employees think he is "the maintenance man." His education stopped at high school, but he was smart and driven enough to make an impact nonetheless. In his high school shop class, he learned how to build. He built a house with his shop teacher and sold it while he was still in high school. And he kept on doing it. He became a real estate developer who now owns a chain of 20 grocery stores, numerous shopping centers, and other properties.

He wasn't happy with the income tax or estate plan he had put together, which is why he was so interested in talking to me when he learned what my profession was. A few weeks later, he came to Columbus to meet my team and to talk about hiring us. He engaged in The UltraVision System® Retreat, and we went deep into what he wanted in life.

He has a lot of money, but money is not high on his list of things he cares about. He lives in a 720-square-foot house… Talk about the "millionaire next door." The first time he told me, I couldn't believe him—a wealthy real estate developer living in a place that tiny? Clearly, he valued humble living. He had strong, prudent reasons for living well below his means.

His net worth was tied up in his business and real estate, so it was not highly liquid. He was unhappy with the insurance policy he'd set up. This man was very intelligent, but not coming from a wealthy or educated family, no one had taught him how to manage his finances. He learned much from the school of hard knocks.

His main "itch" was taxes. As he put it, "I feel like I'm just working for the government."

After taking him through our process, we ended up helping him sell his business to his employees. His kids didn't need it, he didn't need it, and it helped him save an incredible amount of taxes and create a philanthropic foundation to help the communities where his grocery stores are located. That was the brighter future he wanted to build.

He didn't initially have a successor, but now his daughter is involved in the business. We laid out a path that was easy for her to engage in, and she's now in charge of the foundation and has taken some leadership roles in the business. Now, his employees are making more money than would have otherwise gone to the government to pay taxes. Everyone this man cares about is winning thanks to his hard work… It's gratifying for him to know there's a succession plan in place and that his work will carry on after his life is over... And it all started with a plane ride where I almost asked this nice man who needed real help to leave me alone so I could read my book in peace...

CHAPTER 6

The Math Model

What is a math model and why is it important to have a great one?

A good math model gives you a mechanism to make decisions by demonstrating what your numbers could look like in the future if you take a certain course of action. It shows you your current trajectory—which is immensely valuable for determining if the actions you're taking will lead you to your goal. The math model quantifies the answer to the question we started with, "Am I okay?" Will you be okay? Or do you need to make adjustments to your plan?

But many people make big decisions with weak math models…and that's a big problem.

Some advisory firms (generally large institutions) use invisible, back-office technicians to build the math models for advisors to present to their clients. As a result, when the advisor presents the model, which they did not really build, they are not as well suited to help the client understand it. Clients often hand us a plan and say, "See, I have a plan." But when we say, "Okay, tell me what I need to know about this," they can't tell us anything. Weak math models often only focus on a single "issue" and do not combine the other 8 dots of the 9-dot puzzle so to speak. Sometimes they are just done poorly. For example, we've seen tax decisions made using the wrong tax bracket, wrong ages, improper cash flow assumptions, omissions of major tax benefits, and more.

A good math model will show you what's possible after looking at a set of assumptions that make sense to you and to the advisors you trust—and give you something concrete to think about and perhaps share with your accountant or other advisory team members when explaining why you want to take a certain action.

When you place your old plan alongside a new plan you've created that's guided by your Letter of Intent, it's often the first time you will see with great clarity what you want and the reality of how your current actions have or have not positioned you to get what you want. It may be the very first time that what you want and how you're going to get there are deeply connected.

You can use a math model to predict what the next five, ten, twenty years, and beyond would look like with your current plan. Then, you can test your new plan by running it through the math model to see how your future would differ when using the new plan instead of the old plan.

The math model provides a way to test ideas for achieving your goals. A good math model will help you optimize your resources so there's more for yourself, your family, and your community. It quantifies how you're going to make progress and what the steps are to do that.

We'll input your current balance sheet into the math model to assess what you have today. How much money are you earning? What tax strategies might be consistent with your Letter of Intent that would help you net more? What tax consequences are your investments generating each year? How much are you really accumulating? How much are you really spending? A lot of busy successful people think they know the answer to these seemingly simple questions. But when we do the math and add it all up they are often very surprised. Lots of water has flowed over the dam and they have lost mental track of all the details. So with good facts and a math model, it is then that you can quantify the range of what is possible given where you are and your current assumptions and behaviors. What is the upper range of possibilities and what is the lower range of possibilities? Usually, the real answer is somewhere in between.

When you build your math model, you may find that you have 50 or 60 components as pieces of your puzzle. If you can improve just a few of these by just 1%, the compounded effect over time is incredible. Most people are skeptical until they double-check the math.

For example, one optimization opportunity is with insurance. Often, people have the same insurance for years and never look at it to assess if it's still the best option. Sometimes, people don't realize that they're underinsured for liability. To fix this and to save money, we can raise deductibles and increase the upper limits so they have more coverage but pay less. The compounded effect of saving this money over many years often has a large impact.

Another opportunity involves taxes. We don't have all thousands of pages of the IRS tax code memorized, but let's just say we are more familiar with them than most people, and we have a network of experts we tap into who collectively know about all there is to know. Buried in there are traps for the unwary and opportunities for the nimble and the alert. Supreme Court Justice Learned Hand's famous quote says quite a lot about this topic:

> *"Anyone may arrange his affairs so that his taxes shall be as low as possible; he is not bound to choose that pattern which best pays the treasury. There is not even a patriotic duty to increase one's taxes. Over and over again the Courts have said that there is nothing sinister in so arranging affairs as to keep taxes as low as possible. Everyone does it, rich and poor alike and all do right, for nobody owes any public duty to pay more than the law demands."*
>
> -The Honorable Learned Hand, Justice,
> Supreme Court of the United States

Have you arranged your affairs so that your taxes are as low as possible? In today's world, most tax preparers are in the business of calculating your taxes. They do not have the time or rarely have the opportunity to help you "arrange your affairs." So many tax savings ideas are incentives to do or not do certain things. Without a good Letter of Intent that a strategic tax advisor might be equipped with, helping you "arrange your affairs" would be like taking a path at random with no destination in mind– and you may not be so happy about where you end up. Maybe you have had such an experience.

Seeing a great math model that gets you *where you want to go,* can motivate you to take action because you see the future results that the changes you make today could have when compounded over time.

We will use the math model to look at what happens when you optimize each component of your finances.

To optimize your retirement plan, we'll often explore the idea of paying yourself as the director of your own business. Your CPA may initially protest that this would create extra payroll tax, but if you set it up right, you can use director's fees as a source of additional compensation that can qualify for a deduction into an additional retirement plan. If you have discretionary cash flow and one of your goals is to accumulate for retirement and reduce taxes, that could save you money and get you a predictable source of future cash flow in lieu of paying more taxes. Yes, you may be paying more in payroll tax, but you will save much more in income tax. This plan would be tested with your Letter of Intent and a great math model to see if it's the right fit for you.

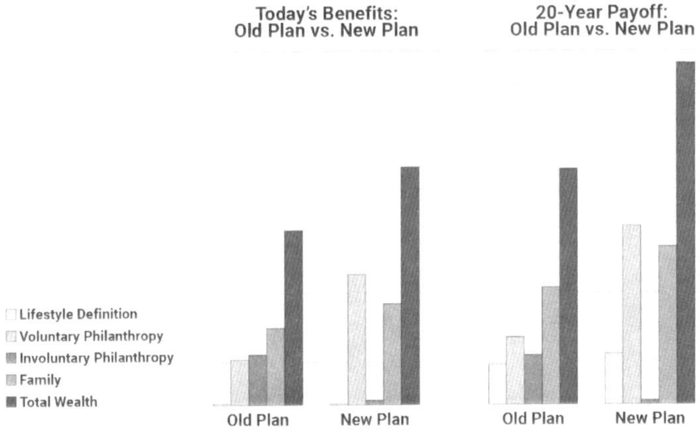

We do interesting math models that often can achieve a zero estate tax plan. Your transfer plans can be designed so that your family ends up receiving 100% of the value of your estate. This can be achieved by trading tax dollars for philanthropy at your death. This is accomplished by making commitments during your lifetime that are not honored until your death. This commitment delivers current tax savings. Those savings are used to deliver a compounded financial benefit to you for the rest of your life. During your lifetime, you can be in full control of the use and investment of your family wealth. Then, at your death, the money that would have been taxable can be transferred to a foundation that your family controls. They can't spend it on themselves, but they can use it to give back to the community. Your kids can use the family foundation that you've established to improve their world in a manner consistent with your dreams, goals, and ambitions (and/or theirs!). Your children may increase their cash flow by never having to dip into their pockets to make any charitable contributions because of what you put in motion for them. A fun win-win-win for you, your family, and your community.

Another option to consider is paying the default tax, but using life insurance dollars to discount the "cost" of the estate tax. Life Insurance can be structured to deliver dollars free from income, capital gains, and estate taxes–triple tax-free. This offers great leverage for reducing the cost of some major taxes. To determine if this makes sense for you, a math model can calculate if there's a life insurance option that would give you significant tax savings and also ensure more of your estate goes to your family.

If you have a business, our analysis has two components: your personal lifestyle and your business. Optimizing the business is usually the most dramatic way we can add cash flow and net worth.

With math models, we drill down to as much detail as we need to make it meaningful. For most people, that means a year-by-year trajectory. But some clients have so much going on that they need a month-by-month math model… Our approach to the models is tailored to your situation.

The bottom line is a great math model empowers your confidence by considering reasonable alternatives and assumptions so you can take action and stay in control of your family wealth while making big progress on your specific dreams, goals, and ambitions.

Law Firm Liquidity Surprise

A few years ago, we were contacted by a CPA who had seen us help many clients save both income and estate taxes.

This CPA wanted us to work with one of their clients who owned a mid-sized law firm in the Los Angeles area. The firm's owner was making a multimillion-dollar income and getting frustrated with the large amounts of checks they were writing to the government for income taxes. As a result, this client decided to engage in The UltraVision System® to explore opportunities for mitigating taxes both now and in the future.

The retreat process yanked this busy legal professional out of his job for 48 hours to think about his future alongside his significant other and determine what they wanted to accomplish.

Their big itch was income taxes. They were not exactly a married couple, but they were happy having lived together for the past ten years. They each had their own financial success and had not commingled anything other than their habitation.

We inventoried the hard facts and found low-hanging fruit.

The company only had a 401(k) plan in place. 401(k) plans generally benefit all employees. The company was contributing. However, the contribution as a percentage of the owner's compensation was capped out by the government and was a very small percentage.

This client, in his early fifties, although working hard and making lots of money, was not on track for financial independence, which concerned him. Most of the value he'd accumulated in life was his paycheck, which allowed him to enjoy a nice lifestyle. Though he was doing a great job accumulating, his lifestyle would never be sustained at the pace he was accumulating. Therefore, in the feasibility phase, we opened up his eyes to an opportunity to retool the retirement plans and continue the 401(k) for most of the attorneys who worked in the office, but to do a supplemental plan that generated income tax savings for him as the owner and allowed him to make large tax deductions for the contributions to the plan that saved him almost a million dollars a year. This money went straight into a plan to benefit him and a select few others. He was to get about 80% of the benefit.

The unfortunate part about these plans is once they are "stuffed" with money, the government limits how much you can put in. Several years later, part of the strategic plan was to break off part of the law firm that did marketing. The reason we did this is you can sell a marketing business, but a law firm does not have a high value, and most states won't allow a lawyer to sell a law firm. So the marketing component of the business was segmented off and, as it turned out, produced a large profit that could be valued by an outsider. This value could then be sold.

The best buyer, as we investigated, turned out to be an employee stock ownership plan. This plan allows the owner to sell the business tax-free.

It also allows debt, which is incurred to purchase the business from the owner. It allows this debt payment to be, in effect, made with the income tax payments the owner was previously making. In order words, redemption of the company with tax payments the owner would otherwise be making. This financial strategy accelerated the financial independence track of the owner and accomplished it in four years, whereas he would have never made it on the old plan track he was on.

Again, the combination of the retreat and an excellent math model incorporating the entire asset base of the client made it ultra-clear what the most effective choices would be for this client. That is why this process is called, The UltraVision System®. Now, a few years after this event took place and the money poured into the client's hands, the client has decided to get married and enjoy additional tax benefits that will enhance his and his spouse's lives even further.

The epiphany they received from the combination of the retreat and the exploration of the math model conversations between the old plan and the new plan were revolutionary.

This client now has UltraVision® and won't stop talking about it! They've been a wonderful source of referrals to the firm for people they know in situations that are not too unlike their old ones. We're grateful for such wonderful people to have come into our lives and to be able to help them.

CHAPTER 7

The ABC's of Cash Flow

Often, people who have a lot of money don't have clarity about how it might be used to optimize their family's cash flow. Money to most seems "fungible" in the sense that it is "all money" and can and should be used for any purpose any time we want to. Organizing various pockets of money for specific purposes can deliver major benefits to families. Doing so can seem complex. To simplify the complex, we've developed a system that has benefited thousands called "The ABC's of Cash Flow™."

While The Math Model provides you with a big-picture strategy, The ABC's of Cash Flow™ gives you a practical way to live with your new plan. It's one thing to show you a graph that predicts what will happen in the future if you take certain actions, but it's another thing to look at that graph and think, "Exactly how am I going to do this?? What does this mean for how I live my life on a day-to-day basis? How does my family survive financially on a daily basis? Where should they get money for specific purposes from? Does it matter? How much of this goes to taxes? How much of this is "fun money" Can I spend as I please? What if something good or bad comes along that I don't expect?"

Learning Your ABC's

A=Available Funds

This money is available to spend today. It is typically kept in a checking account. When you're in the accumulation phase (earning more than you spend), the "A" money bucket will be regularly refilled with your earned income.

You are in the distribution phase when you are spending more than you are earning and you can afford to. In other words, you are in "retirement" or have become financially independent. Distributors refill their "A" accounts with Social Security, pensions, and strategic distributions from their "C" accounts. A great math model helps you understand how much to take, when to take it, and where to take it from in order to optimize your Letter of Intent's dreams, goals, and ambitions.

In designing your A account, a good understanding of your lifestyle definition is required to determine the low and high "watermarks" or level of dollars that should be stored here. These levels help you know when you have too much or too little available to enjoy life the way you want to. If it is too much, it is time to beef up one of your other two accounts. Too little in the account means you will have to tap your buffer account for more. If this happens frequently you will need to rethink the design of your A accounts and perhaps your lifestyle definition. Programming these levels can be done with automation and a good Wealth Management System. Doing so is the beginning of disciplined, goal-oriented, enhanced financial progress.

B=Buffer

Your buffer money is set aside so you're prepared when dangers or opportunities arise. These may be anticipated and unanticipated expenses. Anticipated expenses are large, planned expenses that you know will occur over the next 6 to 36 months. These expenses may be for things such as a second home, a car, college tuition for your child, or tax payments. The buffer account protects your C account from having to be drained or tapped during negative market fluctuations. Tapping your liquid investments during downturns is called negative compounding. Negative compounding can cause large emotional and financial damage. A well-funded and properly invested B account prevents negative compounding. It helps avoid you having to experience negative compounding by protecting your C account from being forced to distribute money at an inopportune time. If your C account drops in value due to some financial crisis or regular market volatility, simply have your B account prepared and "programmed" to tap in such circumstances. B accounts, properly designed and maintained, are one of the key ingredients to empowered confidence and long-term, above-average financial success.

C=Compound

There are two meanings to "compound" in The UltraVision System®.

The first meaning refers to compound interest. Einstein is quoted as saying that compound interest is "the eighth wonder of the world." It can work for you or against you. The

UltraVision System® empowers your confidence by having compound interest work *for* you. Your C money should be compounding or growing in greater and greater amounts over time—it's your financial engine.

The second meaning of "compound" refers to your fortress. It's surrounded by a barbed wire fence, and it's difficult to get in and out of easily.

You can be more aggressive with C money than you can with A money or B money.

These funds are allocated in accordance with your risk tolerance profile or investment policy statement. The allocation is done on a global basis with all your various long-term investments intended to support you in the future. An ideal spend rate as a distributor is 3% or less of your C funds. This is ideal because economists believe if there were no inflation, 3% is all you could earn on money. Spending at this rate will allow your C account to grow during periods of time when earnings exceed 3%. A design such as this can provide the greatest confidence in long-term inflation-protected security. As a distributor, when the inevitable market correction or decline happens and it affects your accounts, your C distributions are turned off until your C account has properly recovered. This is easy and practical to do because you have a properly designed B account.

Before working with us, most people co-mingle their money between these three categories. They think of it all as just "my money" and don't segment it out for many specific purposes. But with the ABC's, we can quantify what you wrote in your Letter of Intent and give you easy parameters that ensure you can accomplish what you want.

In our Wealth Management System, we'll label your accounts as A, B, and C, so it's very simple to get a clear picture of your money and what the specific, simplified purpose of that money is (A, B, or C) at any current moment. "My A money is where I go first...I don't tap into my B money unless I'm out of A money...C is my compound. I won't take anything out of that unless we're intentionally making a big adjustment to my plan or unless I'm in the distribution phase."

Boundaries both high and low are established for your A and B accounts. This puts discipline and confidence into your financial management system. AI and digital workers can be employed to assist in the oversight of this process.

No-Remorse Spending

Some people feel guilty about spending money. The ABC's are designed to remove that guilt. Guilt around spending is usually rooted in a fear of the unknown. People don't have clarity about how much of their money will be needed as a safety net in the future, so they hold back on spending because they're afraid of not having enough. But the ABC's free you to actually enjoy your A money, knowing that you have enough B money and C money set aside. Your A money is designated to be spent with no remorse on having a lifestyle you enjoy. You have a buffer if you get carried away and overspend, and if you underspend, you can spend more tomorrow.

When people use the ABC's, they develop confidence that they're making the best decisions they can with their finances. You can rest easy knowing that you have the pieces on your chessboard on the right squares. This simple system gives you clarity, removes fear of the unknown, and allows you to enjoy the money you've worked so hard to accumulate.

The Summary Opinion Letter™

At the end of The UltraVision System® feasibility phase, we'll give you The Summary Opinion Letter™. This letter starts with a one-page document that summarizes the dangers and opportunities you are facing, under the categories of preserving, building, and transferring your wealth. This summary is followed up with as much detail as is necessary to make sure that you, the decision maker, are able to make a competent, informed decision about each quantified idea.

The letter uses the math models to quantify what you're worth in the short term and the long term. Then, it lists the next steps–and what these steps would mean financially to you and your family if you took action on them both in the short term (less than 36 months) and beyond (more than 36 months)

Referencing your Letter of Intent, the Summary Opinion Letter reminds you of what you said you want to accomplish and outlines a course of action for you to take to accomplish those goals.

With the Summary Opinion Letter, you are empowered to transition from evaluation and feasibility to action.

The Impact of an UltraVision

Some years ago, we took a client and his wife through The UltraVision System® feasibility phase all the way through implementation.

Their itch was that they had two children, one who was in the business and another who lived in a different state and had nothing to do with the business. The son in the business was growing in his responsibility and had shown an aptitude and a capability for having a positive impact on the business. The business was fourth generation. The son of the third generation had grown the business way beyond his father, who had grown it beyond his father. Our G3 client had decided it was time to put a process in place for transitioning leadership from G3 to G4.

During our retreat, the G3 husband and wife made the decision that over the next decade, a turnover would be ideal. Ten years out, the business should continue to grow and the son was showing good leadership capabilities. We crafted an excellent Letter of Intent that detailed their family history as well as their philosophical values, along with their dreams, goals, and ambitions for the rest of their life. The math model depicted their old plan. After we inventoried all of their various assets and their titles, we did a mock estate calculation showing them who would receive what. In particular, between their three major beneficiaries: their family, the IRS, and their children. As it turned out, the IRS was the largest single beneficiary. This proved to be a big motivation to develop a new plan.

One of the dangerous components of the old plan was that if the G3 mom and dad both died, the son and daughter would be 50/50 owners of the business, with the son having worked in it and knowing it intimately and the daughter not having any insights or experience whatsoever in the business. No one thought this was a good idea, but it was the old plan.

After much consultation and discussion, a new plan was drafted and then reviewed by lawyers and CPAs. It required much nudging on behalf of our team of "crickets." Ultimately, the new plan was put in place.

The new plan called for a ten-year run on a gift discounting tool that we called a deferred inheritance trust.

This trust gave control of the business to the son while delivering an equal financial value to the daughter at the end of ten years.

This technique, if successful, would deliver tens of millions of dollars of additional value to the family by reducing the dollars that the IRS would have received.

Many people don't realize that the estate tax is truly voluntary. The IRS has put incentives for successful business owners to develop a succession plan so the business does not die with them. Many business owners ignore this and the business does die.

The risk to this strategy is if the client dies before the end of the ten years, all is for naught. Therefore, the client decided to back up the plan with life insurance to discount the tax should they die prematurely.

Now, the ten years have elapsed and the plan worked! Therefore, the need for insurance has been mitigated.

These dollars can be turned to better uses for the family and business. The son now has control and the daughter has an equivalent value.

The client recently told us how grateful he was for the nudging and The Cricket Factor™ over a decade ago and how it never would have happened without our persistent follow-through, staying on top of lawyers to get the drafting done, and making the plan come to life.

Hundreds of employees are benefiting from the tripling of the value of the company, the son is having more fun than ever, and the parents couldn't be prouder. All because of the UltraVision they got over a decade ago.

CHAPTER 8

The Cricket on Your Shoulder

Do you remember the story of Pinocchio?

Geppetto the puppet-maker was granted a wish by a fairy godmother as a reward for being a good man. He had always wanted to have a son, so the fairy godmother brought one of his puppets, Pinocchio, to life. Geppetto raised Pinocchio as his son. But one day, after the kids at school make fun of him, Pinocchio has a realization: "I'm not a real boy…I'm a puppet made out of wood." The fairy godmother makes a deal with Pinocchio: he can be a real boy if he goes to school, minds his father, and does not tell lies.

But as much as Pinocchio wants to achieve his dream, the world distracts him. The kids at school talk him into skipping class, and soon he's telling little white lies that become bigger and bigger… Throughout his journey, Pinocchio has a friend on his shoulder: Jiminy Cricket, a talking insect who acts as his conscience. As Pinocchio deviates from his "plan" Jiminy Cricket asks him, "Pinocchio, don't you want to be a *real* boy?" Eventually, the persistence of the cricket helps Pinocchio change his ways and focus on his big ambition. Jiminy Cricket has no real power over Pinocchio—Pinocchio could and did flick him off his shoulder a few times when he was annoyed by his questions. At the end of the day, the decisions are Pinocchio's to make. But throughout the story, Jiminy Cricket's questions and reminders end up being the path for Pinocchio to achieve his big dream.

Like Pinocchio, we all have dreams. But sometimes, the world distracts us and we get off track. Many times, we know what we need to do to reach our goals, yet we don't do it because the distractions of the world get to our heads. The role of the cricket is to be a steadfast guard against these distractions, always there with a gentle nudge: "Remember what you want in life. Remember what your purpose is. Remember to take the next tiny step towards making your dreams come true."

We aim to be the cricket on your shoulder. Your decisions are in your hands, but we'll be there along the way to say, "Wait a minute. Are you sure that's the choice you want to make? Will this path lead you to your goal? Or did you change your mind about your goal?" The world is designed to distract. Those with good "crickets on their shoulders" have the best chance of making their dreams come true.

The basis of our long-term client relationship is managing a plan to keep you on track with your Letter of Intent. "Remember in your letter you said you wanted to be a real boy? The fairy godmother told you the recipe to achieving that dream. Here's the recipe. Do you want to make the choice that follows the recipe to achieve your dream or the choice that will take you further from what you want?" The cricket doesn't have the same emotional attachment to your decisions that you do, so it can be a more objective voice.

There's always the possibility that your goals shift, and you want to change the Letter of Intent. If this possibility arises, we'll help you look in the mirror and assess whether you've changed your mind or if you're just straying from the path toward your goals.

In Chapter 3, we discussed the studies that concluded that the most successful graduates were those who put their goals in writing and then shared their goals with someone who supported them. That's our role—by sharing your goals with us through The UltraVision System®, we become your personal cheerleader, your Jiminy Cricket, who is there to remind you of the goals you set and will celebrate with you when you achieve them. Our success ends up being a fraction of your success.

Defeating Procrastination

A 2019 psychological study concluded that procrastination is a significant contributor to poor financial progress. In a 2010 book on the science of procrastination, researcher Piers Steel found that 95% of people procrastinate some of the time.

When it comes to financial success, procrastination is likely your #1 enemy. You know what you need to do, but the trouble is actually doing it. Many people think, "Oh, I'll do it tomorrow"... Tomorrow, they think, "Oh, I'll do it next week"... Next week, it's "Oh, one of these days I'll get around to it."...And then they never do. My accountant-client may never have started real estate investing. My restaurateur may never have moved, expanded, and tripled her business.

When the stakes are as high as they are in financial planning, procrastination can have devastating consequences. What happens if a business owner who thought, "Oh, I'll get to it one of these days," suddenly dies, and the family loses their fortune because the owner didn't have a plan in place? What happens if a business owner wants to retire and realizes, "Oh...I would have been much better off if I'd prepared for this years ago"?

To achieve the dreams you wrote about in your Letter of Intent, you have to defeat procrastination...

You could try to overcome procrastination the hard way—by exerting your own willpower. But you've likely tried that for years or decades with mixed results.

If someone has trouble sticking to a workout regimen, a common solution is to hire a coach. The simple fact of having someone to hold you accountable makes it possible to avoid procrastination and accomplish your goals. The same strategy works for your financial goals...

The cricket is like your personal trainer in the world of money, only better. The cricket power includes help getting things done and leverage to get them done. With regard to your finances you can, but you don't have to "do all the work."

The cricket is the engine that propels you forward on your chosen path. On a monthly, quarterly, or annual basis, the cricket will measure the distance between where you are and where you want to be—and remind you to take the next step forward. And at every crossroads, the cricket will be there to say, "Remember what you want… Here's where each path will lead. Which will you take?" Then you can empower the cricket to do things for you, so again, you don't have to.

The Power of a Cricket

Years ago, I had a client who was a successful contractor. I was helping him put together a transfer of wealth plan that involved life insurance. As I sat with him and his family in their beautiful home in a nice neighborhood, he pounded his fist on the table so hard that the water glass sitting on it went flying. He screamed, "I don't owe anybody anything, and I'm not starting now!" He was sixty-five, had never owned life insurance, and didn't want to commit to paying a premium every year. It felt like a loan to him.

Like Jiminy Cricket, I didn't back down. I calmly said, "You don't have to do it. But if you don't do it, here's what will happen after your death." I laid out how much the government would take in taxes after his death. "Yes, you'll be spending $50,000 on insurance, but your wife and kids will get to keep your business and real estate instead of losing it to the IRS. It's your choice: the government or your kids." He decided to purchase the life insurance.

Years later, he becomes ill, and his death is imminent. He calls a meeting to go over the estate plan with me, his lawyers, his accountants, and his family. His death would not be free from income and estate taxes. His estate had grown. His life insurance helped greatly, but it wasn't enough. It did make the difference between keeping the family business and not losing it to the IRS.

He saw what this tool was about to do for his family and was surprisingly glad he had taken up what he did. Then he looked at me with a long, serious face and said quietly this time, "Why didn't you make me buy more?" His family and I burst out laughing—we all remembered that day when he pounded his fists on the table and yelled at me. But fifteen years later, this man had regret about not taking our full advice. The life insurance he did have, which I recommended on that day, made the difference between losing everything he'd worked his whole life to build and keeping it in the family. Without a cricket, this man would have had much more to regret—and his family would likely not be laughing.

Buying life insurance was a highly emotional decision for this man. He needed an objective voice of reason to lay out the facts so he didn't get carried away by his emotions and failed to understand how this decision would impact his family. That's the power of a cricket.

Another client, Joe, was a corporate executive at a successful, closely-held business that had about 350 employees in three states. He was told by the owner that if he did a good job and stuck around, someday, the owner would sell him the business. As it turned out, two other people were told the same story. A horse race…

This young man had come referred to us by another young man who was a successful salesperson for this business. This fellow was told the same story by the owner. They liked each other, so they decided they would try to buy the business together. I was introduced to the pair to try and help them develop a strategy for convincing the owner to sell to both of them instead of just one. For a variety of reasons, that wasn't a legally acceptable option.

The second executive, who had a nice home, a car, a little 401(k), some savings, and a decent paycheck, but really no significant net worth, ended up hiring us to work with him and his wife to develop a strategy to make the most out of this situation.

The business was quite successful, but Joe had a vision for exponentiating the growth.

He wanted the fellow who introduced us, Carl, to be his partner, but the owner wouldn't have it. So we went to work.

In the end, Joe won the horse race. He was given the opportunity to purchase the business, but only by himself. Yet he wanted Carl as a contributing teammate/partner.

We helped him craft a deferred compensation agreement, a customized benefit plan for Carl so he could have the benefits of ownership without legally owning any of the business. In essence, he would be Joe's phantom partner.

When we conducted the retreat for Joe, he and his wife, like so many others, had never spent 24 hours over a two-day period thinking about the future of their finances and how they wanted to connect it with their family. They found it a very exciting strategic opportunity.

Joe was very good at setting goals, achieving them, and then rewarding himself for the achievement. We inventoried these goals and played Jiminy Cricket over time. The first was a Rolex watch that he would purchase when the company hit a certain sales goal. He'd never had one.

He could have afforded one in the past, but he'd always wanted to wait until he did something significant. Buying the business and growing it significantly qualified!

He went on to set numerous goals, which we played the cricket for. Reminding him when he got distracted. Helping him keep score over time. And then having the funds available to satisfy the various rewards he wanted when he got to the next level.

Over 25 years, we helped Joe hit certain personal goals, family goals, and business goals, ultimately exiting at a relatively young age and enjoying life the way he and his wife wanted to, traveling, seeing their grandkids, boating, and much more.

The punchline to this story is that Joe brought his son, Tommy into our office not too long ago to do financial counseling with one of our advisors, Maureen. Tommy has been out of school, was getting married, and had a decent job with some discretionary cash flow. Tommy had a clue that his dad had been ultra-successful. More than one or two clues…

As Joe listened to the advice being dished out, Tommy questioned what he should do. Joe said, "Just listen to what Maureen is telling you. How do you think I became so successful?!" There is no better endorsement of The UltraVision System®.

It's experiences and comments like this that make what we do fulfilling and help us see the impact of it…that having an independent third party oversee the dreams, goals, and ambitions of a driven person can amount to something very special for everyone.

CONCLUSION

When your financial plan doesn't take into account your big-picture goals in life, it's like you're headed on a road to nowhere. You might end up somewhere...but you may not like where you end up.

Do you want to keep heading down that road? Or do you want to get clarity about where you want to go and build a plan that will help you get there?

When you know you're on the path toward what you want in life, you'll be at peace. You'll no longer sit up at night wondering, "Am I okay? Am I missing something? Is there anything else I could be doing to improve my finances?"

And with a quality advisor as the "cricket on your shoulder," you'll no longer be the only one responsible for keeping track of your finances. You can focus on running your business, and/or building your career, pursuing your ambitions, and making memories with your family while we keep an eye on the road to make sure you're on track with your goals. If there's an obstacle up ahead, we'll notice it before you do, and we're always on the lookout for new opportunities to leverage.

Average people can have average financial planning. But you're not average—you're one of the few great people. You want to have a larger-than-life impact on this world. You always have an ambitious goal to pursue. You need a financial plan that's focused on your unique purpose in the world, not just on numbers and dollar signs. Let us be the cricket on your shoulder while you focus on being great.

The UltraVision Story

Joseph and Carmela Antolino were impoverished immigrants who struggled to come to America in the 1920s to make a better life for themselves and their children. Ralph Antolino Sr. was born shortly thereafter in Columbus, Ohio. His father had a job laying tracks for the railroad, and his mother built a small restaurant business serving railroad workers food and beverages. It was across the street from the railroad roundhouse where the workers came and went to work and where the family lived.

Carmela and her husband could not read or write Italian, let alone English. It was a big handicap but did not stop them from sending all three of their children to college to become teachers. Carmela revered teachers because not only could they read and write, but they could *teach* others how to read and write. Ralph Sr. was a revered teacher at Gahanna Lincoln High School for five years. During that time, his income grew to $2,000 per year. Not per month! It was not much money even then. He struggled to feed his growing family. An older fraternity brother of his encouraged Ralph

Sr. to begin selling life insurance part-time in addition to his teaching, which he loved.

It did not take long for Ralph Sr. to make more money with his part-time job than his full-time occupation, so he quit teaching and started Antolino & Associates, Inc. in 1960. The business began with a strong emphasis on "teaching" clients principles that helped them *preserve, build, and transfer* wealth. This emphasis persists today.

Ralph Jr. joined the firm in 1975 as a college student. Working at his dad's business, Ralph Jr. became inspired by his father, along with the business professors at The Ohio State University (OSU). As an honor student, he became president of the OSU Insurance fraternity and obtained dual majors in finance and insurance. The vision expanded to include a tax law degree to better help successful business people optimize their wealth because so many large decisions had tax implications that people didn't understand or get good advice on. The vision combined various tax and financial strategies that crossed the disciplines of legal, accounting, finance, and insurance. The vision evolved into The UltraVision System® which has become the firm's flagship unique process. This process today adds great value to successful business owners, complementing traditional advisory services and allowing these owners to get greater value from what they have already developed in their lives.

Now, the firm has thousands of client relationships, several offices, and deep relationships with clients and other professional service providers across the United States and abroad. We are driven today to constantly improve our ongoing value proposition to busy, successful clients through The UltraVision System®, which helps The few great people that we work with get clearer and clearer about where they are, where they want to go, and the choices they have for getting there. All the while helping clients become and stay better organized, better relating to their dreams, goals, and objectives, and more in charge of their financial affairs.

We help successful people by delivering The UltraVision System®. It is a time-tested process that Empowers Confidence™ for business owners who want to preserve, build, and transfer wealth.

BONUS CHAPTER

Trading Tax Dollars for Philanthropy

The UltraVision System® is designed to optimize your family's financial values through a multi-dimensional planning process that starts with the end in mind.

Successful planning is much more than simply looking at a net worth statement, tax tables, and running the numbers. There are four distinct dimensions to every family's wealth: financial, social, emotional, and spiritual.

The financial aspect of a family's wealth is the most shallow, impersonal, well-defined, easiest to discuss, and least important of the four dimensions.

Ninety percent of all planning currently being done begins and ends at the financial level. Traditional planning is nothing more than a series of unpleasant business decisions that have to be made to minimize the damage.

The social aspect of a family's wealth is more complex, moderately personal, not well-defined, more difficult to discuss, and very important.

Traditional planning shies away from the social aspect of wealth. Yet when we connect your wealth to your social desire to improve your community by trading tax dollars for philanthropy, incredible things happen.

When you pay taxes, who controls the distribution of your family capital? The government.

When you use The Ultra Vision System®, we now allow the family to include the social aspect, which is a more efficient use of social capital. We all know that the government isn't the best business person. Using your money for charity rather than paying taxes ensures that your money isn't wasted and that you send your dollars to causes you care about.

Using your money to make a difference in a way that honors your values leads to high fulfillment—and you'll have a stronger motivation to implement your plan because it's tied to something you care deeply about.

The introduction of the social variable into the planning equation produces exciting new planning options.

But we don't stop at the social dimension… We also want to explore the spiritual dimension.

The spiritual aspect of a family's wealth is personal and more difficult to discuss. Many advisors are afraid to delve into this dimension, yet it's critically important. How do your beliefs impact your financial decisions?

The UltraVision System® also explores the emotional aspect of a family's wealth.

The emotional aspect of a family's wealth is extremely complex, extremely personal, almost totally undefined, difficult to discuss, but critically important. This aspect takes most advisors way out of their comfort zone.

But if we fail to explore the social, spiritual, and emotional dimensions, we fail to address the deep nagging question at the center of human life: "Will my descendants and the world remember me after I'm gone?"

Ernest Becker wrote, "This is mankind's age-old dilemma in the face of death: what man really fears is not so much extinction, but extinction *with insignificance*. Man wants to know that his life has somehow counted, that it has left a trace, a trace that has meaning. And in order for anything once alive to have meaning, its effects must remain alive in eternity in some way."

What's the point of financial planning if your wealth is disconnected from your life's mission? How can we use the money you've accumulated to build a legacy after you're gone?

Most people live what we call a compartmentalized life. They take these 4 dimensions separately.

The financial aspect of life is a desire to be independent, to be able to do what you want to do and to have the money to do it.

The social aspect of life is about helping others in your family and your community.

The emotional aspect of life is about the desire to feel significant.

And finally, the spiritual aspect of life is about the desire to find immortality.

Most people run around these circles like a baseball diamond, faithfully touching all the bases, but as a result, when they follow this compartmentalized approach, there's usually something out of balance. One of the circles may get bigger than the others.

Ultimately, something feels missing, and people ask, "Where's my life purpose in this? What am I doing it all for?"

Synergizing your life mission starts with expanding all of these circles to their maximum capacity and looking for what we call the fire within, the part of your life where all these dimensions of your life converge. This is your passion.

Writer George Bernard Shaw said, "This is the true joy in life… being used for a purpose recognized by yourself as a mighty one… I am of the opinion that my life belongs to the whole community, and as long as I live, it is my privilege to do for it whatever I can. I want to be thoroughly used up when I die. The harder I work, the more I love. I rejoice in life for its own sake. Life is no brief candle to me. It's a sort of splendid torch which I've got to hold up for the moment and I want to make it burn as brightly as possible before handing it on to future generations."

Growing a strong family tree and igniting your "fire within" are two of the more important components of a great family mission statement, and skillfully blending these four distinct dimensions in The UltraVision System® produces unique and powerful solutions.

So how do we trade tax dollars for philanthropy?

First, we have to understand family wealth. What most people don't realize is that their multi-million dollar net worth is divided into two parts: your social capital and your personal capital. In other words, the part you can't keep and the part you can keep.

Our laws say you have to reinvest in your community and the world to make things better, roads, armies—taxes. Most people are familiar with the idea of income taxes. But at your death, your estate is divided into two more parts, the part that goes to the IRS and the part that goes to your heirs. I encounter some very charitable people, but when I ask them if there's any charitable component in their estate plan, they say, "Oh, no, if my kids want to give something to charity, they can do that." People don't want to take anything away from their heirs because they already have to give a portion to the government. As a result, a lot of very philanthropic people give nothing to charity.

But what if instead of disinheriting charity, we disinherit the IRS? As a result, by committing to do that during your lifetime, you end up with more personal capital because there are tax savings for you while you are alive for making this commitment. With those tax savings and the benefit of time, your kids actually get more money, and because there is time, we can compound that, and that box can be as big as your original net worth. What's fascinating is charity doesn't get exactly what the IRS gets. They can get more.

In summary, we take your multi-million dollar net worth, multiply it over your remaining lifetime, increase both the personal and social capital, and eliminate the government as a beneficiary of your estate.

This is all done under the control of your family. We know that entrepreneurial people are better at managing where dollars go than governmental institutions, so many business owners are excited by the prospect of letting their family control it instead of the government. You can now maintain maximum control over both your social and your personal capital. A lot of people never thought about managing their social capital beyond their lifetime, but it's possible. In summary, you can pass the entire value of your estate to your kids without paying any estate taxes.

"Hang on…is that really possible?" some of you may be thinking, "Do you mean to tell me it's possible to pass the entire value of my estate on to my kids without paying any estate taxes? Do you mean to tell me it's possible to sell my appreciated assets and not pay a dime in capital gains taxes? Do you mean to tell me it's possible that, after avoiding all these estate and capital gains taxes, the IRS is going to give me an additional current income tax deduction for opting out of paying these taxes? Do you mean to tell me it's possible to become a multimillion-dollar philanthropist, supporting numerous charitable and social activities, and actually end up wealthier in the process? Do you mean to tell me it's possible to do all this and not end up in jail?"

The answer to all of these questions is an emphatic "Yes!".

And now we'll show you how…

Case Study: Mr. and Mrs. Pills

Mr. Pills is an extremely successful owner of a pharmacy that delivers customized compounds across the U.S. He had bought the pharmacy from his father twenty years earlier and took this small business and built it into a quite substantial regional company.

Mr. Pills is 53 years old with five children. He wanted to semi-retire from a full-time, active role in the business in three years and begin turning over the management of the company to his one son who was in the business, and another key employee.

He had accumulated 5 million dollars in his company pension plan.

He wanted his one son and the key employee to become the owners of the company. He also wanted to treat all five of his children equally with their inheritance.

He knew if he sold the company to his one son and the key employee, he would face devastating capital gains taxes on the sale. If he waited to give the company to them at his death, his family would face even greater devastation from estate taxes.

Mr. and Mrs. Pills were not particularly philanthropic people. They were, however, personally involved in a number of charitable activities in their small Midwestern community.

Our challenge here is to:

- Eliminate the oppressive taxation on his pension funds at the second death
- Help show them how to successfully keep the family pharmacy in the family without being crippled by capital gains or estate taxes at the time of transfer
- Help them eliminate all their estate taxes
- Help them leave to the other four children an inheritance equal to the value of the pharmacy they want to leave to their one son

The result?

Their net lifetime income went **from $12 million with the old plan to $19 million with the new plan.**

The benefits to the family went **from $11.2 million with the old plan to $24 million with the new plan.**

With the old plan, they would pay $11 million in taxes at death, but **with the new plan, they paid nothing in taxes and contributed $26 million to charity at death.**

Just imagine how much impact the Pills family could have in their community contributing $26 million to charity.

How do you want to be remembered? As a taxpayer who involuntarily had it taken away, or as a philanthropist who voluntarily gave it away?

The choice is yours.

NEXT STEPS

If you are ready to start your UltraVision journey there are two paths:

1. You can download worksheets and checklists and implement it yourself. Simply navigate to https://Antolino.com/bookresources or scan the QR code.

2. You can engage with one of our highly skilled advisors, who will walk you through every step of The UltraVision System® so that you are assured of the very best experience, and most complete plan for fulfilling your UltraVision. Simply call (614) 442-3355 or email contact@antolino.com.